WAREHOUSE WILLIE TEAMSTERS STEWARD CHRONICLES

CALEB CARTER

DEDICATIONS:

This book is dedicated to all the hard working shop stewards around the world

Illustrated by Patrick Harrington
harringtoon@gmail.com

Special thanks to Lisa Brennan
kitty.callie@yahoo.com

Readers can leave comments, share their union stories,
and their personal shop steward experiences at
warehousewillie@mail.com

ABOUT THE AUTHOR

CALEB CARTER was born in New Orleans, Louisiana. At the age of seven he moved to South Central, Los Angeles with his family. Some of the characters for Warehouse Willie were inspired by his Teamsters Union co-workers.

I RESENT BEING CALLED LAZY FREDDY! YESTERDAY I WORKED ON SEVEN MACHINES!
HOW MANY DID YOU FIX?
THAT'S NOT THE POINT. YOU'RE SUPPOSE TO FIGHT FOR ME REGARDLESS!
SOME UNION MEMBERS TAKE ADVANTAGE OF THE SYSTEM...
...AND SOME GO ABOVE AND BEYOND TO EARN THEIR BENEFITS.
LIKE GETTING OUT OF BED ON A COLD MORNING WHEN YOU REALLY WANT TO SLEEP!
YEAH, NOTHING TOPS THAT, FREDDIE.

WILLIE, I SAW YOU DISCUSSING UNION BUSINESS ON COMPANY TIME!
THAT WAS PERSONAL BUSINESS, ED
YOU CAN'T DISCUSS PERSONAL BUSINESS ON COMPANY TIME!
WHAT CAN WE DISCUSS ON COMPANY TIME?
ONLY COMPANY BUSINESS ON COMPANY TIME!
IT WAS PERSONAL BUSINESS ABOUT THE COMPANY
THE UNION... COMPANY... PERSONAL... FORGET IT. IF I WRITE YOU UP YOU'LL FILE A GRIEVANCE TO MAKE ME LOOK STUPID
I BELIEVE YOU BEAT ME TO IT ED

ED, DID YOU DO THE ANALYSIS I ASKED FOR?
YES SIR
WE NEED 98% WAREHOUSE REPAIR AND 2%EMPLOYEE PRODUCTION IMPROVEMENT TO GET NEW BUSINESS.
LET'S RIDE OUR EMPLOYEES NINETY EIGHT PERCENT HARDER.
THAT'S NOT GOING TO INCREASE BUSINESS.
NO, BUT I'LL FEEL BETTER ABOUT NOT GETTING IT.

FIRST VIOLATION OF COMPANY POLICY IS INSUBORDINATION. YOU DO WHAT I SAY OR I CAN FIRE YOU.
OKAY, YOU ROCK HEAD FOOL!
DISRESPECT IS IN THE POLICY TOO!
WE HAVEN'T GOTTEN TO IT YET, SO EAT IT, JERK!
LET'S SKIP DOWN TO INSULTS
HARRINGTON '15

YOU'RE FULL OF EXCUSES, WILLIE. IF I SAY A UNION MEMBER WAS SLEEPING ON THE FLOOR, YOU SAY HE PROBABLY SLIPPED
IF I SAY A UNION MEMBER DIDN'T USE THE EQUIPMENT PROPERLY, YOU SAY IT WAS PROBABLY BROKEN.
THIS TIME A UNION MEMBER IS APPARENTLY DRUNK IN A CHAIR. AND YOU SAY--
MAYBE HE'S JUST HIGH
PLEASE DON'T HELP ME!

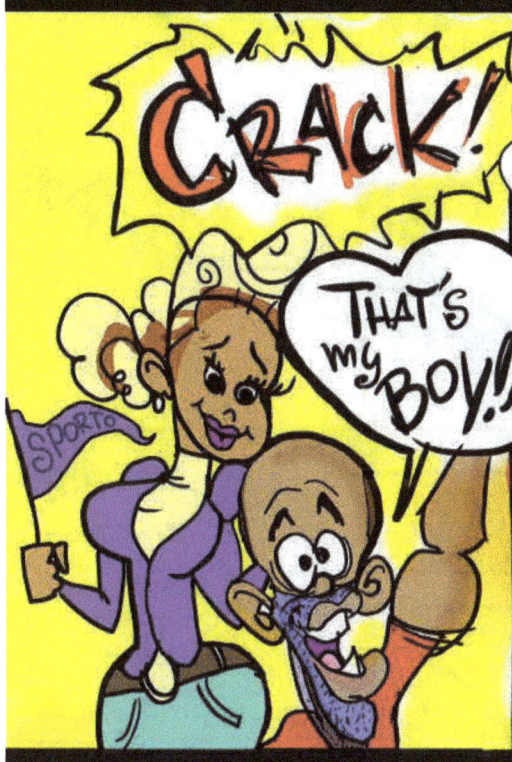

THESE UNION MEMBERS ARE TAKING THIS CONTRACT NEGOTIATION WAY TO SERIOUSLY. YESTERDAY SOMEONE SNUCK ON BOARD MY YACHT AND STARTED A FIRE.
IT SOUNDS LIKE THEY'RE TRYING TO FORCE YOU BACK TO THE BARGAINING TABLE.
INSURANCE WILL COVER THE DAMAGES, BUT I MAY HAVE TO RETHINK MY STRATEGY.
ARE YOU GOING TO NEGOTIATE IN GOOD FAITH NOW?
MAYBE I'LL BECOME MORE STRINGENT SO I CAN BUY A NEW YACHT.
DO YOU FIND IT HARD TO BE SO UNSCRUPULOUS?
A CRUISE ON A NEW YACHT CURES A LOT OF GUILT.

I DID A VISUAL INSPECTION DURING LUNCH AND FOUND TWO CANDY BARS AT YOUR WORK STATION. THEREFORE I'M GIVING YOU A VERBAL WARNING.
I HAD THREE CANDY BARS AT MY STATION.
WOULD YOU PREFER A WRITTEN REPREMAND?
YOU'RE RIGHT. IT WAS TWO.
NO, ON SECOND THOUGHT THERE WAS ONLY ONE.
CANDY

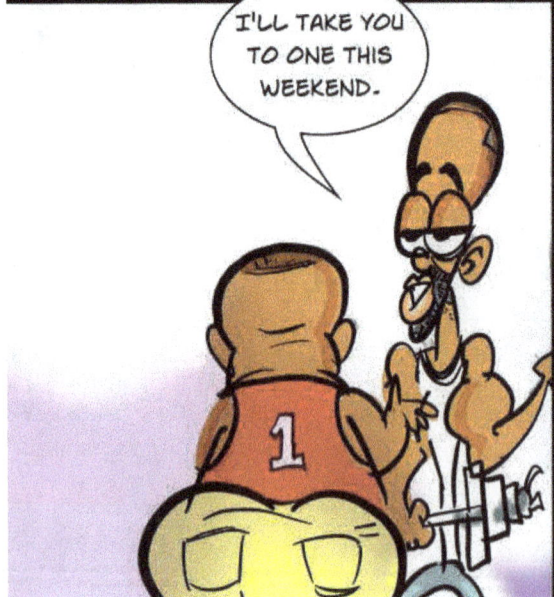

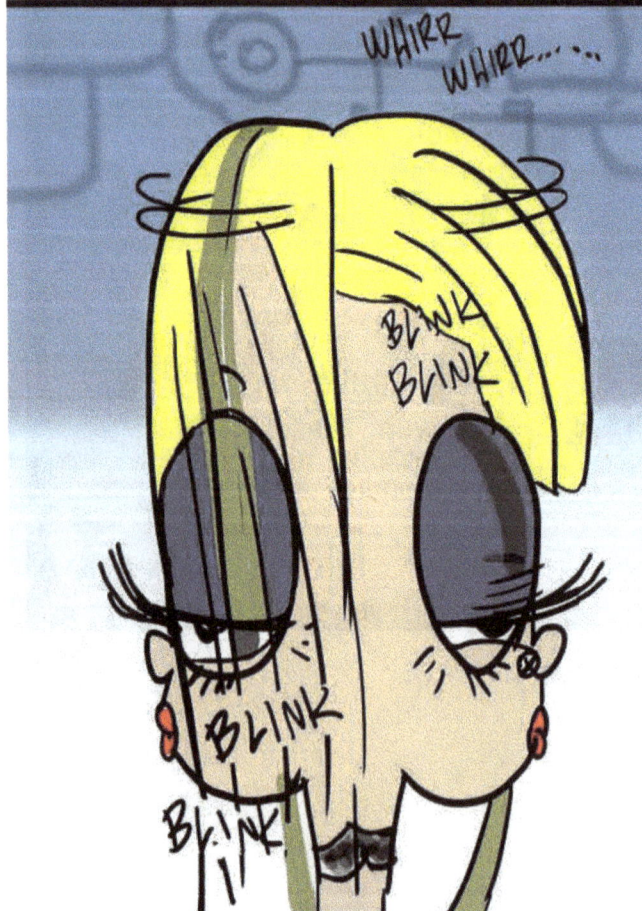

OTHER BOOKS
BY
CALEB CARTER.

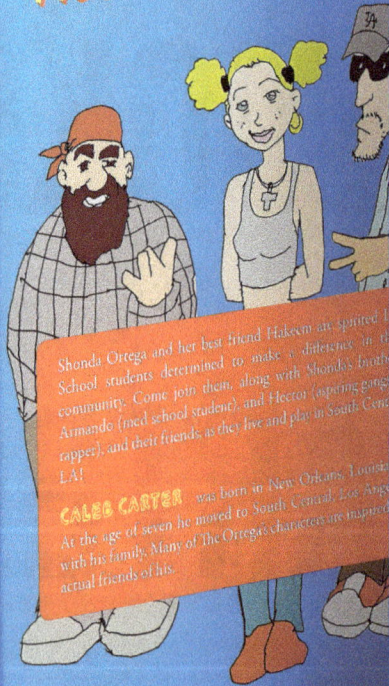

MEET THE ORTEGA

Shonda Ortega and her best friend Hakeem are spirited High School students determined to make a difference in their community. Come join them, along with Shonda's brother Armando (med school student), and Hector (aspiring gangsta rapper), and their friends, as they live and play in South Central LA!

CALEB CARTER was born in New Orleans, Louisiana. At the age of seven he moved to South Central, Los Angeles with his family. Many of The Ortegas characters are inspired by actual friends of his.

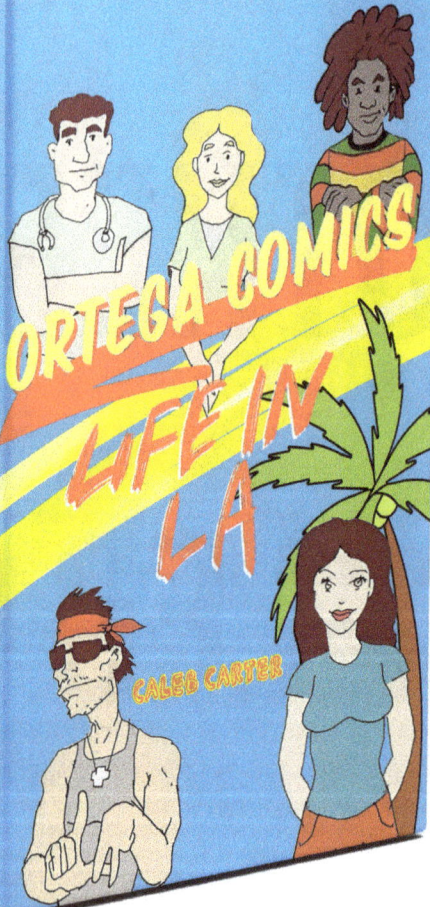

ORTEGA COMICS

LIFE IN LA

CALEB CARTER